A WOMAN
WITH VISION

A WOMAN WITH VISION

HOW TO FULFILL THE GOALS
AND DREAMS GOD HAS GIVEN YOU

L'areal Lipkins

Copyright © 2019 by L'areal Lipkins

L'areal Lipkins

Spring, TX 77379

www.AWomanWithVision.com

Book Layout ©2017 BookDesignTemplates.com

Cover Photo: Quintan Lipkins/Clutch Images

Cover Design: Camden Lane Creative

Illustrations: Mauve Paper Co.

Ordering Information:

Quantity sales. Special discounts are available on quantity purchases by corporations, associations, and others. For details, contact the "Special Sales Department" at the address above.

A Woman With Vision/ L'areal Lipkins—1st ed.

ISBN 978-0-578-46312-4

This book is dedicated to my Grandma Pearl who made me fall in love with reading at four years old, my Big Mama whose strength and resilience runs through my veins, and my mom whose love has always been unconditional.

Listen to your vision
What does it say?
Though it is small and still
Let it lead your way
When all else fails
Let its loyalty stand
And fight alongside you
Protecting the purpose at hand
Within a desolate desert
Let it quench your soul
In the midst of dead winter
Let its fire dispel your cold
Let it beckon you forward
Though your steps may bring fear
With faith and endurance
Your fulfillment will near

CANDACE OKIN

Contents

Introduction   9

Shadows   13

There's Levels to This   24

The Goal Setting Trap   40

Creating Clarity   47

Planning & Execution   57

Mindset: The Belief Gap   71

Elevating Your Mindset   81

The Myths of Motivation   93

What's Your Motive?   101

The "F" Words   108

Who Must You Become?   122

Go to Work   138

Acknowledgments   151

Introduction

Have you ever had that feeling deep inside that says, "It's got to be more to life than this?" I know that feeling all too well. But for years, I ignored it. Even though I wanted more, secretly, I didn't know if I was capable of more.

The truth is that I had grown comfortable playing it safe. In fact, *safe is better than sorry* was a mantra I lived by. But then one day, I decided that life was too short to play it safe. I decided that I was going to go after everything that I desired as if winning was the only possible outcome. *Writing this book is a result of that decision.*

Chances are you're reading this book because you too have big dreams. Dreams of sharing your story with the world, thoughts of launching that business, dreams of starting a nonprofit, or dreams of being able to buy what you want, when you want. *Amen!*

Perhaps you see yourself traveling the world experiencing cultures you didn't even know existed. Maybe you want to go back to school, or rebuild your self-confidence after an abusive relationship. Regardless of what your goals are, I want you to know the only thing getting in the way of you accomplishing your goals is you.

By changing one mindset, you have the power to change the whole trajectory of your life. By developing one skill, you can impact the lives of thousands. By making one decision, you can go from dreaming to actually doing.

In this book, I will be sharing lessons learned on my journey to become a woman with vision, and I believe every word will speak to the woman with vision inside of you. In the process, I hope it will do more than merely inspire you, because inspiration is short lived. I want this book to push you to take action, because taking action is what causes you to manifest all that you desire.

Throughout this book, you will find questions and exercises, and I know it will be tempting to skip over them. Don't! These exercises are meant to help you apply the information immediately. Remember, it's not inspiration that creates change, it's implementation.

Lastly, I pray this book awakens every dream that you forgot about and every goal that you've abandoned. I pray that it reignites your passion and pushes you to say "Yes" to your purpose. I pray that it gives you the courage to expand your idea of what's possible. *And, I pray that it helps you unleash the power within that comes from being a woman with vision.*

Much Success,

Lareal Lipkins
Wife, Mother, Visionary

CHAPTER 1

Shadows

*Create the highest, grandest vision possible for your
life, because you become what you believe.*

OPRAH

"Mom, Mom, Mommy!" he screamed as he came running into the kitchen.

"Moooom! Help!"

At first, I thought he was just playing, but I quickly realized that he was truly terrified. For a second, I thought maybe our dog, Bella, was chasing him, but she was looking just as confused as I was.

"Mom, pick me up!"

I immediately stopped cooking, and tried to figure out what was going on. That's when I saw it. It was his shadow.

As the light of the kitchen met the darkness of the living room, it created a shadow. At two years old, it was the first time our son had seen it, and because it was unfamiliar, it scared him. To try to calm him down, I began to explain to him that his shadow was just a bigger version of himself, but he was not having it!

Truth be told, you and I have all found ourselves in this *same* situation. Maybe you weren't two years old, perhaps you were twenty-four and in a period of trying to discover who you were. Or maybe you were thirty-six and searching for significance and meaning. Or you might have been forty-eight and thinking about the next phase of your life. Whenever it was, we've had *that* moment—the moment where you're just living your life and you catch a glimpse of your shadow, the bigger version of yourself. The version of yourself that genuinely believes that anything is possible and has the guts to go after what you really want versus what you've been settling for. The version of yourself that decides to color outside of the lines and makes no excuses for it.

JUST THE BEGINNING

In 2015, I saw my shadow for the first time. At the time, I had been working at a sales training and consulting company for six years. I had gone from being a part-time marketing intern to director of marketing to managing partner, and there were even talks about me buying the company soon.

But then God started showing me a bigger version of myself. He showed me traveling the world speaking to thousands of women about raising their standards and mindset. When I watched television shows, I would imagine myself in the guest chair doing interviews and answering questions from the audience.

I would listen to a podcast and practice the questions I thought I would be asked if I were a guest. By the way, these weren't conversations I was having in my head. These were conversations I was having with myself out loud like it was nobody's business! Because it wasn't! Even then, I knew the importance of mentally seeing myself win. This is what we call visualizing or forecasting the reality you want to create.

You have to see it in your mind, before you see it in your hands.

In the vision God showed me, I saw my husband and I giving away college scholarships. I saw us paying off all of our debt in full, one by one, without having to check the bank account balance.

One day, I was even walking through the Austin-Bergstrom International Airport in Austin, Texas, and as I walked past a bookstore, I saw a book with my name on the cover sitting on the shelves. The vision was so lifelike that I did a double take just to make sure I wasn't going crazy. What's so funny is that this was a couple of years before writing a book was even on my radar. God is funny like that. Sometimes He will reveal things to us before we're even thinking about it so that when it happens, we know it was Him. I'm convinced that He was showing me my shadow!

Something was exciting about this bigger version of myself, but I was also scared. Although I never had any intentions on being in sales, much less working at a sales training company, after five years in the industry, I had developed a network.

People recognized me as a sales expert and speaker. I was working with clients that I enjoyed working with, and I was making multiple six figures as a twenty-something year old. So instead of embracing this bigger version of myself, I did what my two-year-old son did ... I ran.

ON YOUR MARK, GET SET, GO...

Running can show up in several variations. For some people, it may be Denial. Denial means you deny yourself the ability to think about your vision or goals too long because you don't want to get your hopes up. Some people use denial as a defense mechanism because they've set goals in the past that they didn't achieve, and they don't want to feel the sense of disappointment again. So instead, they limit themselves to things they are certain they can do. Unfortunately, in the process they sell themselves short by settling for what's safe.

For others, it may be Minimizing. With Minimizing, instead of talking about what you want to accomplish as a realistic goal, you talk about it as something you would like to do "someday" if you ever get the opportunity. A common sign of minimizing is giving a disclaimer like "I know this is big, but..." before sharing your goal with someone. When people minimize what they want to do, they're usually in between having a wish and setting a tangible goal. My preferred method of running was logic.

Who would leave a job making multiple six figures when you have a mortgage, two car notes, and a two-year-old?

How are you going to find clients?

How are you going to get insurance?

What are your clients going to think?

So are you going to throw away the last nine years?

Are you really as good as you think you are?

You have some major deals that are about to close, can't you just wait and see what happens?

These were all questions I asked myself to try to justify staying where I was.

Logic is a silent dream killer.

I was a master at using being "responsible" as a reason not to take action. And yes, you don't want to make rash decisions. But if you look at people who achieved significant success, they all went against the grain. They made decisions where they had to bet on themselves. It doesn't matter what your goals are, you won't accomplish them if you only do what makes "sense."

I'M NOT TOUCHING YOU!

Fortunately, everywhere I went, my shadow followed me. One day, I was doing a speaking engagement for a group of CEOs, and I was wrapping up the Q&A portion. I did the last call for questions when one of the attendees asked me what I thought about having employees put together a vision board.

Now, you know I wanted to jump on my soapbox, but I couldn't because I was still working at my corporate job and that's what I was there to talk about. So I kept it simple and said, "I think vision boards are a great tool to help people create a visual of what success looks like for them ... and it also works well with getting clear on the department and corporate goals."

This didn't just happen once. If it had, I probably would have blown it off as a coincidence. This same question came up four times in the last six months I worked at my corporate job.

It was as if God was reminding me of where He was taking me and who I *really* was. If that wasn't enough, things started to happen at my job that really began to get under my skin.

At first, I tried to consider it a tradeoff for all the money I was making. But when it started to affect my health, I knew I could no longer put a price on my peace. November 12, 2018, I stopped running and I resigned.

Was it scary? *Absolutely!* Did people think I was crazy? *I'm sure.*

But what was scarier was the thought of looking back at my life wishing I had gone for it. Maybe you've found yourself in that place too. God has shown you a bigger version of yourself but you're scared because you don't feel qualified or ready.

Sometimes it's not about being ready, it's about being willing.

One thing I've learned is that when you're willing, God will always make sure that you're ready. Now, before you start writing your resignation letter, I want to be clear. I'm not suggesting you leave your job just because you don't like your manager or the dress code policy. Nor am I suggesting you make any other life-altering decisions right now. What I am saying is, don't let fear keep you from living your dreams out simply because where you are is familiar. You have to be able to recognize when you have gotten comfortable in a place that was only meant to be temporary. I thought I was going to be *buying* the company, but God said, "No, I'm preparing you to *build* a company."

The nine years I was at my corporate job was training ground, and I will forever be grateful for what I learned and who it pushed me to become. However, God was calling me to another place, and He knew the only way to get me to shift was to get me uncomfortable.

Your shadow is unique!

Only you know the vision and dreams God has placed on the inside of you. Ask God to give you discernment and wisdom on the best time to go after your dreams, and then go for them!

TAKE ACTION

What does your shadow look like?

When did you first see your shadow?

How did you respond?

A woman with vision owns who she is.

CHAPTER 2

There's Levels To This

> *If one is lucky, a solitary fantasy can totally transform one million realities.*

MAYA ANGELOU

I was twenty-one when I was first introduced to formal goal setting and vision boards. And to be honest, I had no clue what I was doing. One Saturday afternoon, I went to the store and bought a stack of magazines. I spent the rest of the day cutting out quotes and pictures that "inspired me." I glued them on my poster board and thought... *Let's see if this vision board stuff really works.* Fast forward twelve months ... NOTHING happened!

That's when I realized that if I wanted to be a master at setting and accomplishing my goals, it was going to require more than creating a cute collage. In fact, the "magic" of the vision board has nothing to do with your actual board, it's what you do before and after that makes the difference.

If you don't have a clear vision of what you want, a vision board won't help you!

When done correctly, your vision board should be your roadmap for the year. You should be able to see exactly what you want to focus on for each quarter. That means gluing random pictures all over the place isn't going to work. Your vision board should be organized and have 80% pictures, and only 20% words. Why? Because your brain loves pictures! Yes, a picture really is worth a thousand words. For example, if you want to buy a house, don't put the words *Buy a House* on your vision board. Find a picture of a house that you want to buy, go take a picture of yourself and your family in front of it, and then put *that* picture on your vision board. I guarantee you will get there much quicker!

THE SQUEEZE

After totally butchering my first vision board, I spent the next five years and a lot of trial and error, figuring out a goal-setting process that really worked for me. I would set a goal and knock it out. I would pick another goal and knock it out!

As a result, my life and lifestyle started to look a lot different than sleeping on my mom's couch. I had gone back to school to get my MBA, traded in my Altima for a Mercedes; I was winning awards, making money, got married, and we were preparing to buy our first home.

By society's standards, and mine at the time, I was living the life! But inside, I was unhappy. You could even say I felt empty. I had a yearning for more. Not more stuff, but more fulfillment. More significance. More purpose. It was during this season that I learned that...

Goals without vision leads to frustration.

Up until this point, I hadn't even thought about *vision*. In fact, I didn't even know there was a difference between vision and goals. I was so busy chasing material things that I never stopped and thought about where I was headed or who I was becoming.

In the social media addicted world we live in where everyone is "faking it 'till you make it," having a real vision for your life has never been more critical. You have to have your own definition of success that reflects who *you* are and what *you* value. If you don't, the world will sell you a dream that will never satisfy you.

People define vision differently, but for the purpose of this book, I want you to think of vision as

An image of your life in the future.

SEE IT BEFORE YOU SEE IT

Vision is long term and often intangible. Sometimes the vision has to do with your overall purpose and calling and other times it's a vision for a specific area of your life. Let's look at the first type of vision.

A few years ago, I had a dream that was so vivid it was scary. In the dream, I was speaking on stage in a jam-packed theater. As I closed my speech, the audience erupted into cheers and gave me a standing ovation. I looked around smiling, teary-eyed, and I thanked them for their graciousness. I walked off stage and there was my husband standing behind the curtain holding our baby. I told him, "On to the next one," as we headed to the next city.

When I had the dream, I hadn't done any public speaking, I wasn't married, and didn't have a baby. I had that dream over four years ago, but anytime I second-guess myself, I think of that dream. I truly believe God was showing me a vision of what's to come, and I can't wait for that dream to manifest.

The second type of vision, which is what we want to focus on, has to do with a specific area of your life. What's the vision you have for your health, career, business, spiritual growth, marriage, family, and finances, just to name a few?

This type of vision is where you dream on purpose. Instead of having a dream, you create the dream by clearly defining your idea of success and then intentionally creating a life that aligns with that vision.

The challenge that many people have with vision is that they're so attached to their now that they can't visualize their next.

SOMETHING LIKE MICHELANGELO

To be a woman with vision, you have to be able to see beyond where you are now. It's like being a sculptor of your own destiny. A sculptor can take a block of material that looks insignificant, unimpressive, and useless to everybody else, and create something that is not only beautiful, but lasts for hundreds and thousands of years.

Where you are right now is just *part* of your story, not the end of it. With every step you take, you are literally chiseling away at the block of stone. You have to hold the finished picture in your mind, which can be difficult if you're not in a pleasant place. But if you shift your focus to *learning* from your current situation versus just trying to *leave* your current situation, you will see that there's some molding and character building that needs to take place. You will start recognizing habits and ways of thinking that have been keeping you stuck. You will learn what you need to do differently in the next phase so that you will be able to sustain whatever it is you desire.

This is what I experienced in the last eighteen months at my corporate job. I felt like I had been more loyal to a company than I had been to myself, so my initial reaction was to become fixated on all the negative things that had transpired.

That's when God told me to shift my focus. Instead of focusing on "them," I needed to work on me. Looking back, I see there was molding and shaping that God was doing in that season. There was some bitterness I needed to let go. There was some pride He needed to chisel away. There was some insecurity He was working out of me that I didn't even know I had.

Yes, I know the people on your job are frustrating you, learn patience. I know you're tired of trying to make ends meet, learn discipline. I know you want to provide a better living situation for your family, learn how to monetize the skills you already have.

All I'm saying is, where you are right now will teach you what you need to know for your next chapter if you're willing to learn from it. If you're not, you run the risk of taking old attitudes and behavior into what's supposed to be your new season.

SLOW DOWN TO SPEED UP

Another challenge we have with vision is that we are impatient. Be honest! You want everything right now! But you're not going to get everything in *3 Easy Steps!* And you should be thankful for that. If vision is being able to see beyond where you are, that means your vision is bigger than where you are. And if your vision is bigger than where you are, it's probably bigger than WHO you are right now.

Time gives you the grace to grow into who you will need to be to carry out the vision. Stop trying to rush the process, and stop trying to force it. What God has for you doesn't have to be forced, it flows. Some visions you have will happen quickly, others will take time. Embrace the journey. The only thing worse than getting something before it's ready is getting something before *you're* ready.

#GOALS, I THINK

We've talked about vision, but let's switch gears and talk about goals.

Goals are things that move you forward.

This is important to know because social media will have you thinking anything you want is a goal and it's not. Goals should advance you, help you get to the next level, and foster growth.

Buying a handbag is not a goal. Getting a luxury car is not a goal. Going on expensive vacations is not a goal. Notice I did not say you can't have them, just know that they are not goals. They are rewards.

I make this distinction because it is easy to get wrapped up in material things that add no actual value. If you accomplish a goal, go ahead and take a vacation. If you close a significant deal, buy the designer handbag. That's fine! Just get them in the right order.

CONNECTING THE DOTS

Unlike vision, goals are tangible. You know for a fact whether or not you accomplished your goals.

When your goals and vision are aligned, your goals become the building blocks for your vision.

For example, if you have a vision that your marriage is going to be restored and the passion is going to be reignited, you might be able to see that in your mind. But to see it manifest, you need to set some goals that will support that becoming a reality.

Some tangible goals you might set are:

- Weekly date day/night
- Daily one-on-one time
- Quarterly get-away
- Attend a marriage conference or retreat

Again, you don't have to guess whether or not you accomplished your goals, either you did or you didn't. The same process can be applied to any vision. Let's pretend your vision is to be financially independent. You would need to set some tangible goals that support your vision.

Some tangible goals you might set are:

- Save 10% of your income
- Pay off credit cards
- Save three months of monthly expenses
- Increase income by $1,000/month

The point is that you need to have both vision and goals. Let me show you what it looks like when you have one without the other.

VISION WITHOUT GOALS

If you have a vision and no goals, you say things like:

I want to practice more self-care.

I want to travel more.

I want to be more confident.

While you might have the best intentions, chances are you won't accomplish much because there are no specific goals tied to it. And if you do make an improvement, it will be far less than what you could have achieved if you had set a measurable target.

Typically when people have vision without goals, it's because they've never been taught how to set goals. They don't know what they don't know. Now, let's take a look at people who were like me: tons of goals but are lacking vision.

GOALS WITHOUT VISION

If you don't have vision, it is very likely that you feel all over the place or unfulfilled. You might even be accomplishing a lot of things, but they don't seem to bring the joy and excitement that you thought they would. Let me give you an example that might be familiar.

Have you ever been getting ready for a trip and you decide you want to lose five-ten pounds before you go? So, for the next few weeks, you are on your best behavior to make sure you look good on South Beach.

Congrats! You lose weight. And then what happens when you get back from vacation? You gain the weight back and then some (or maybe that's just me)!

Why does this happen? This happens because you had a goal of losing five pounds, but you didn't have a vision of having a healthier lifestyle.

That's why I say there's levels to this. The first level is having a vision or long-term picture of what you want. The second level is your goals, which when executed should get you closer to your vision. Level three is all about celebrating your progress by treating yourself with a reward. This is what I call the Vision Goals Rewards Pyramid

TAKE ACTION

Write out the vision you have for the following areas. Once you write out your vision for each category, write out 1-2 goals you want to get accomplished for each area. If some areas don't apply or aren't at the top of your priorities, skip over them.

SPIRITUAL

Vision:

Goals:

FAMILY/MARRIAGE

Vision:

Goals:

FINANCIAL

Vision:

Goals:

PHYSICAL/MENTAL HEALTH

Vision:

Goals:

BUSINESS/CAREER

Vision:

Goals:

SOCIAL/COMMUNITY/GIVING

Vision:

Goals:

PERSONAL DEVELOPMENT

Vision:

Goals:

A woman with vision knows what she wants!

CHAPTER 3

Goal Setting Trap

If you don't like the road you're walking, start paving another one.

DOLLY PARTON

While some of the goals you wrote down at the end of the previous chapter may have been new goals, there probably were a few that you wanted to complete last year, and the year before that, and the year before that.

Don't worry, this is a judgment-free zone!

I want to let you in on a little secret. The reason you keep recycling some of the same goals year after year is that you're stuck in a trap that you didn't even know existed. It's the same trap that 92% of people who set goals get stuck in, myself included.

Let me give you the behind-the-scenes on what's happening. Whenever you set goals, I'm willing to bet that you start off really MOTIVATED and focused. You are on an emotional high, and there's nothing that can get in between you and the finish line.

This will be the year that I will get in shape!

This will be the year that I will blog consistently!

This will be the year that I will read my devotional!

That motivation causes you to take ACTION. You get up early to do your workouts; you're drinking more water, meditating, counting calories—the whole nine.

The first two weeks you are killing it! You're such a machine, you wonder why you didn't do this years ago. But then week three comes. Your alarm goes off, and instead of jumping out of bed, you take a deep breath mystified at how time went by so fast. It seems like you *just* got in bed and now it's *already* time to get up.

Irritated, you roll over and set another alarm to go off in ten minutes. But instead of going back to sleep, you spend the next ten minutes negotiating with yourself.

You: *I have been doing so good, I've got to keep it going.*

Also You: *I have been doing so good, missing one workout isn't a big deal.*

You decide to come up with a compromise. You won't skip working out altogether, you'll just go after work. Five o'clock comes around, you rush home to change and head to the gym, but you end up in a staring contest with the TV, and you're determined to win.

After a few hours, you check the time.

Wow, is it 7:30 p.m. already?

You decide that you should probably go ahead and cook dinner because you don't want to eat too late, and you'll workout really hard tomorrow. To make yourself feel better, you do a few squats and crunches while your food is cooking.

Before you know it, one missed workout turns into three months of couch surfing. I call this phase: DISTRACTION. You get distracted by your own excuses, responsibilities, and life.

Once you realize that you're nowhere near where you thought you would be, you get FRUS-

TRATED. You wonder why you keep starting and stopping, only to start and stop again! You sulk for a few days, but then you're able to muster up the MOTIVATION to start again.

Rinse and repeat. Ask me how I know!

Even if your goal was something different than getting in shape, we've all found ourselves in this vicious routine. This process is what I call the **Goal Setting Trap**™.

I discovered the Goal Setting Trap™ during those first five years of trial and error that I mentioned in the previous chapter. Any time I would set a goal that really stretched me to change my habits, I could do it for a couple of weeks, but then I would end up right back where I started.

Initially, I was embarrassed, because it seemed like everyone else around me was making moves. However, as I started talking to people about their goal-setting journey, I realized they were going through the exact same thing I was. Yes, they were accomplishing some goals, but when it came to the goals they had to grow into, they were struggling just as much as I was.

Part of me was relieved to know that I wasn't the only one who felt like I was failing. The other part of me couldn't help but wonder why this was happening to begin with. After reflecting on my own story and those of the people I talked to, I noticed a glaring pattern.

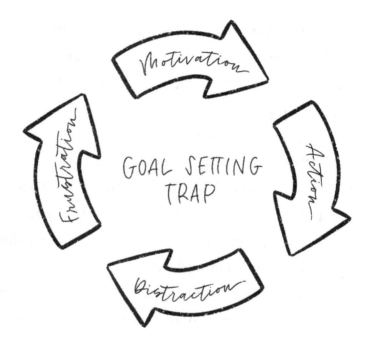

Does this pattern sound familiar?! Not only is the Goal Setting Trap™ insanely frustrating, but it can also make you start doubting if you'll ever be able to accomplish your goals. *Maybe you should lower your expectations*, whispers insecurity. And because you don't know what else to do, you start listening and believing that maybe you've missed your window of opportunity.

It will never happen for you.

You don't deserve it.

You don't have the skills.

You don't have the time.

You don't have the discipline.

Let's be clear, those are all lies! It doesn't matter how long you've been trying to accomplish a goal, know that...

God's promises never expire.

Your whole life can change in a year. Matter of fact, your whole life can change in the next second. That doesn't mean that it's going to be easy. Anything that's worth having always requires work and consistency.

Now that I've shown you what's been holding you back, I can give you the roadmap on how to move forward.

TAKE ACTION

When's the last time you were stuck in the Goal Setting Trap™?

What did you learn about yourself now that you know about the Goal Setting Trap™?

A woman with vision is unstoppable.

CHAPTER 4

Creating Clarity

Clarity is the most important thing. I can compare clarity to pruning in gardening. You know you need to be clear. If you are not clear, nothing is going to happen. You have to be clear. Then you have to be confident about your vision. And after that, you just have to put a lot of work in.

DIANE VON FURSTENBERG

Now that we know that traditional goal setting causes us to end up in the endless cycle of hoping and wishing, let's take a look at what we can do to stay out of the game.

When you are working on bringing your vision to life, you have four areas to focus on: Clarity, Planning & Execution, and Mindset. If you fail to address one of these areas, it's safe to say that you will find yourself back in the Goal Setting Trap™, and we both know how that works out.

CLARITY

The most critical word in real estate is location, location, location. Location is so important because it is a huge factor in determining the value of a piece of property. For example, the same 2,000 square foot single-family home that cost you $200,000 in Dallas will cost you $1.2 million in Los Angeles. Why would the same house cost you a million more in LA? Just because of the location!

When you are working toward your goals, the most significant word is clarity, clarity, clarity! Just like the location determines the property value in real estate, clarity determines your ability to fulfill your vision. Anytime you don't have clarity, you have noise. Noise creates confusion, which makes it difficult to make a decision, so you don't. Instead, you toggle between goals, and you end up stuck. Let's define clarity before we dive deeper.

Clarity is about being clear and specific.

There are three areas that you want to have clarity around:

Where you are now

Where you desire to be

How you plan on getting there

WHERE YOU ARE NOW

Let's be honest. Acknowledging where you are can be downright uncomfortable, especially if you know it's on the opposite end of the spectrum of where you'd like to be.

When my husband and I were going through premarital counseling, one of the topics we discussed was finances. I knew that finances would be a talking point, but I didn't expect it to come up so early in the process.

Our pastors walked us through the basics like tithing, creating a budget, and life insurance. Everything was fine until we were given our homework assignment. The assignment was to go over our individual finances together so we could start building a sound financial plan. As the words came out of our pastor's mouth, I felt a wave of emotion come over me, and I seriously thought I was going to pass out.

I knew I had bad money habits, but my fiancé didn't know I had bad money habits ... and I wanted to keep it that way. At the time, my relationship with money was so dysfunctional that I didn't even open my credit card statements. My issue wasn't that I didn't make enough money, I just didn't know how to properly manage it. Now I was going to have to share that with my fiancé, and I was mortified.

A few days passed, and we completed our homework assignment. Once I got through the initial embarrassment, we had a candid conversation about our individual finances. Even though it was extremely uncomfortable, that exercise helped us decide who was going to handle the finances, what debts to tackle first, and how long it was going to take.

It's similar to your GPS. The purpose of your GPS isn't to tell you where you are, it's to tell you how to get to your destination. But the only way it can tell you how to get your destination is by *first* determining your current location.

Your issue may not be money, but regardless, you have to be really honest with yourself about your current status before you can change it.

WHERE YOU DESIRE TO BE

The next area of clarity is identifying where you want to be. This is the area where you get to let yourself dream and create a picture of your future. Although this area might feel better than thinking about your current situation, you might find it just as difficult to find clarity.

That's because a lot of people set goals that are vague. For example, you might have the intention to start your own business. While it is an excellent goal to have, because it isn't specific, your brain doesn't buy into it. When your mind doesn't buy into it, it doesn't see it as a priority in the present, and it becomes difficult to create a realistic plan.

However, if you said that you want to start a graphic design business by March 31st that will generate $5,000 a month in revenue, you have now added clarity to your goal. Notice that I've included a way to measure your goal (revenue) and a time-frame (March 31st). The more laser-focused your goals are, the easier it is to formulate a plan to make it happen.

Not only that, you will know for sure whether or not you accomplished your goal by March 31st. Remember, your goals should be as specific as possible.

> *There is no guessing or wondering if you hit your goal because you have defined what success looks like.*

Leverage + Alignment

The second part of clarity when thinking about where you want to be is to align your goals with your vision. I mentioned this earlier, but I want to give you more detail on how to do it effectively.

Sometimes when I'm doing clarity calls with clients, they come to me with all of these goals they want to work on. But then I start asking them how each goal connects to the broader vision they have for themselves (or God has shown them), and there is entirely no connection.

Now, every single goal doesn't have to connect back to a broader vision, but when it does, it creates leverage. The beauty of having leverage is that if you hit one goal, it propels you forward with three other goals because they're tied together. Instead of working hard, you're working smart. And instead of being confused about which goal you should work on first, you have a sense of focus.

Let me give you a personal example. I shared with you that one of the visions God has given me is that I'm going to travel the world speaking to women. That vision is going to require me to be in the best physical shape I can possibly be in so I can deliver a presentation without being winded. It's going to demand that I'm spiritually filled so I'm able to hear clearly from God about what opportunities I should say yes to and which ones I should pass on. It will also require me to focus on strengthening my marriage and finding time to make sure we stay connected. It also means that I will be able to generate additional income to achieve my business and personal financial goals.

So when I'm working out, I'm thinking about how this workout is going to help me have stamina when I'm traveling around the world speaking. When I wanted to give up on this book, I was reminded of how many thousands of lives would be changed by the words I was writing at one o'clock in the morning. When I'm presented with speaking opportunities, I make sure it includes travel expenses for my husband and son if I'm going to be gone for multiple days. I could go on, but I think you see my point. Alignment gives you the ability to leverage your time, energy, and effort.

If your goals are all over the place, your life will be all over the place. If your goals are linked, everything is in sync.

HOW YOU PLAN ON GETTING THERE

The last area you need clarity about is your course of action. Please note this is the third area, not the first. If you start trying to figure out the "how" before you've even committed to your destination (the what) or understand your motive (your why), you are going to get discouraged.

You must first decide that you are dedicated to achieving your goal by any means necessary. Too many people make the mistake of "trying" to hit their goals.

I'm going to *try* to write a book.

I'm going to *try* to start a nonprofit.

I'm going to *try* to read ten books this year.

Stop trying. Stop "giving it your best shot." And definitely stop saying, "We'll see how it goes" as if you have no control over your life. From this moment forward, decide that you will!

I *am* writing and publishing my book.

I *am* starting my nonprofit.

I *am* reading ten books this year.

This isn't about semantics, it's about ownership. You can do anything if you decide you want it bad enough. And if you're really honest with yourself, there may be some goals you had in the past that you wanted, but you weren't willing to do the work for it. That's okay! Now you know that success doesn't happen by chance, it happens by choice and you can start to choose differently.

Okay, so now that you've made the commitment that you're going all in this time, let's take a look at how to create a blueprint to achieve your goals.

TAKE ACTION

Which of the three areas do you need the most clarity?

Why did you pick that area?

A woman with vision is intentional!

CHAPTER 5

Planning + Execution

The most difficult thing is the decision to act, the rest is merely tenacity.

AMELIA EARHART

If you recall, the first step of the Goal Setting Trap™ was *motivation* followed by *action*. What is missing in between those two phases is a PLAN. You have to take time to create a plan before you start taking action, otherwise, you might be taking action that will lead you in the opposite direction. Creating a plan means you break your goals down to individual steps you need to take with a timeline attached to it.

Typically when it comes to planning, people fall into two categories: wingers and over-thinkers.

If you are a winger, you love flying by the seat of your pants. You might even brag about being able to think on your feet, go with the flow and figure things out as they come up. While all of those things are beneficial assets to have, you really get to leverage them when you have a roadmap in place.

If you're not a winger, you might be more of an over-thinker. Over-thinkers spend hours putting together elaborate plans. The problem with over-thinkers is their need to create the "perfect" plan prevents them from actually implementing it.

The only way to perfect a plan is to put it into action.

Notice I did not say the only way to create a perfect plan is to put in action. There is no perfect plan. Let me repeat that. *There is no perfect plan!*

Take pilots, for example. When you're on the plane flying from Atlanta to New York, the pilot spends most of their time course correcting and making adjustments based on the conditions. Reaching your goals is no different. Once you create a roadmap that's at least 75-80% done, you can shift from planning to execution.

CAUTION: AUTOMATIC DOOR

However, I want to remind you that this is for the goals that you have set for yourself. I make this distinction because you might also have some visions that God has given you. When God has implanted a vision in your heart, He doesn't always give you all the steps you need to take. In fact, He usually *never* gives you all the steps. He does that intentionally. In those situations, God wants to build your faith and dependency on Him.

> *As you take a step, God reveals the next step.*

It's similar to walking through an automated door. If you're sitting in your car just thinking about going into the store, the automatic door does not open for you. The door doesn't open until you get out of your car, walk through the parking lot, and get close enough for it to sense that you're ready to enter.

If God has placed a desire in your heart, and you know that it was God, stop praying for clarity and start praying for obedience. Trust that as you move forward, God will guide your footsteps and open the doors that need to be opened. But you have to make a decision to start walking.

PROCRASTINATION

Have you ever created a plan, but then you kept revising it over and over because it was never "good enough?" That's what I call sophisticated procrastination. You've convinced yourself that you haven't started because you're still planning, but subconsciously you're still planning, so you don't have to start.

> *Beware of procrastination disguised as preparation.*

You often hear about procrastination talked about as the problem, but I believe procrastination is really just a symptom of something else. That something else might be a lack of commitment, fear, taking on too much at once, or even a lack of confidence. But instead of dealing with the real problem, people like to say they are still working on their plan or they're a horrible procrastinator.

If you want to uncover what's really causing you to stall, start paying attention to the tasks you keep putting off and the ones you tackle immediately.

See if you can find a pattern or common thread between the two groups.

- Are the things you keep putting off outside of your comfort zone?
- Do they require you to ask for help?
- Are you scared of what might happen if you follow through?

Once you identify what's at the root, you can start working on the real problem.

Another way to help you stay out of planning paralysis is to set a deadline to complete your plan. You can change your plan as much as you want during that time, but once that time is done, you have to move to the execution phase. Secondly, you can also include a re-evaluation phase in your plan . The re-evaluation phase is when you include a time within your plan to re-evaluate whether or not you are on track. Including this phase in your plan keeps you from making premature changes.

Lastly, when creating your plan, begin with the end in mind. It is much easier to work backwards because you relieve the pressure of tying to get all the steps in the right order. Once you get all the steps on paper, then you can put them in order of what you need to do first.

EXECUTION

Your plan is only as good as your ability to execute it. With that said, let's take a look at how to turn your plan into progress. The biggest challenge I hear from people when it comes to execution is getting started. This might be true for you as well.

Let me give you some tips that will help:

There is no substitute for doing the work.

The quicker you accept this truth, the quicker you will accomplish your goals. Even if you have a mentor, coach, or accountability partner, you *still* have to do the work.

The work is what gets you from a dream to reality. If your goal is to get a certification that will make you more marketable in your field, you have to sign up for the program, pay your fees, go to class, take your test, and pass the exam.

Depending on your goal, there might be things that you can delegate or outsource, but there will always be a piece that only you can do. When I wrote this book, I outsourced the editing, purchased templates, and hired a really handsome photographer (a.k.a. my hubby) to capture the cover photo. But I still had to write the book.

You might be thinking, *That's great for you, but I don't even know where to start.* Start with the easiest step that you can control. For example, with this book I had no idea what I was doing. I could have gotten wrapped up in a lot of rabbit holes like how it needed to be formatted, edited, and distributed. But I didn't. I focused on the easiest step I could control without having to do a lot of research, which was simply getting my thoughts on paper.

I promise that if you stop overthinking it, and you just start working toward your goals, you will figure out everything you need to know along the way. Don't allow yourself to get into the weeds by focusing on things that aren't immediately relevant.

START SMALL

Don't try to take massive action that you're not going to be able to sustain. Instead, take small steps every day and watch them add up.

And don't buy into the notion that you don't have enough time or that you're too busy. The reality is that you don't need more time, you need more focus. I tell my clients to spend 60 minutes a day on their goals. That's roughly 30 hours a month, 360 hours a year. Can you imagine what you could accomplish if you were investing 360 hours a year toward your goals? There wouldn't be a single goal you couldn't achieve!

FIRST THINGS FIRST

If you're like me, you have a secret obsession with to-do lists and post-it notes. You get an emotional rush making a list of the things you've got to get done for the day, and you get a deep sense of satisfaction every time you get to check something off.

As a result, you fill your list up with everything you need to get done, and you always feel worn out and behind as you stare at the five hundred things you didn't get to.

Sound familiar? If so, my name is L'areal Lipkins and I'd like to welcome you to the *Doing Too Much Support Group!*

This is a support group for women, like myself, who insist on stressing themselves out by setting unrealistic expectations of what they can get done in an eight-hour day. In other words, we just Do. Too. Much!

Seriously! I don't know why we do this to ourselves. It's a never-ending cycle of being overwhelmed and anxious. I think I was addicted to this routine because I didn't understand the difference between being busy and being productive. I felt good looking at all the things I needed to get done, until I realized there was *absolutely* no way I was going to get it done within the timeframe I set.

So let me share a tip that I got from the book *The One Thing* by Gary Keller. Instead of thinking about everything you could get done for the day, focus on the one thing you *should* get done for the day that would have the most significant impact on getting closer to your goals. And if possible, do that one thing first. This simple concept completely changed my way of thinking.

I still have my list of everything I need to get done, but now I use it as a master list that I can reference when I'm planning my day. Asking myself what's the one thing I should get done that would get me closer to my goals helps bring the most important thing I need to do into focus. Sounds like clarity if you ask me!

ELIMINATE EXCUSES

You get an excuse! You get an excuse! You get an excuse! Everyone gets an excuse!

There is no shortage of excuses. Excuses are easy to come by and people give them out freely. But the thing about excuses is that they are really expensive.

> *Your excuses today, cost your results tomorrow.*

I encourage you to start paying attention to your go-to excuses. What are the excuses you have on speed dial? Once you're able to identify them, you can start eliminating them.

CELEBRATE YOUR SUCCESS

Some of your goals are short term, meaning you can accomplish them in the next six months. Others might be long-term goals that will take you eighteen months to complete. Either way, you want to make sure that you celebrate as you take small steps, so you don't get distracted and end up back in the Goal Setting Trap™. If you have to wait eighteen months to feel like you're successful, it's likely that you're going to lose steam. But if you've identified seven milestones, critical mini goals, in your plan, that gives you seven opportunities to celebrate.

Celebrate might mean you treat yourself to a reward like we talked about in chapter 2, or maybe you just pause and pat yourself on the back. In my case, it means warm chocolate chip cookies from Tiff's Treats®, but do what works for you!

DEAL WITH DISTRACTIONS UPFRONT

If you break the word distraction down, you get dis-traction. Dis- is a prefix that means the opposite of. Traction means forward progress.

So distractions are people, places, and things that cause you to move backward instead of forward. Social media is one of the more prominent distractions, but your environment may be a distraction. If you work best in an environment that's quiet versus a lot of background noise, you need to find a place that allows you to focus. If you do your best work in the morning but you keep trying to work on your goals at night when you're tired, that is a distraction. If you find yourself changing your plan every time you listen to your favorite podcast, that podcast just might be a distraction. Or at the very least, you should consider setting up some boundaries for yourself.

When I work with clients, one of the things we plan for is any roadblocks that might get in the way. When you think about your roadblocks or distractions up-front, you can plan for them versus being blindsided by them.

DRUMROLL, PLEASE ...

The biggest distraction of them all is the negative thoughts playing in your head. Learn how to silence the counter-productive chatter and align your thinking with where you want to be, not where you are. We'll spend a whole chapter on mindset so that's all I'll say about it for now.

What I've learned most about execution is that we make it way too hard. In our heads, we tend to play out the worst-case scenario. And the worst-case scenario typically never happens. And even if it does, it's just an opportunity to learn how to take a different approach moving forward. Nothing more, nothing less!

As you think about your ability to execute, I want to remind you to just focus on the next step. Don't clutter your mind thinking about something that is five steps away, because all it will do is distract you from the *one thing* that's most important now.

TAKE ACTION

What are some of your go-to excuses?

Pick one to eliminate immediately!

A woman with vision works her plan!

CHAPTER 6

Mindset: The Belief Gap

It is not primarily our physical selves that limit us but rather our mindset about our physical limits.

ELLEN J. LANGER, PHD

It started out just as a small crack here and there, nothing noticeable unless you were really looking for it. But then the little cracks became bigger, thicker, and more apparent. I knew we were in trouble when the doors would no longer close, the crown molding began to separate from the wall, and the hardwood floors began to lift.

We had been ignoring the signs long enough; we needed a foundation repair. So I reluctantly began calling foundation companies to set up an inspection to see how bad the damage was, and more important, how much it was going to cost.

The first company came out two weeks later and delivered the news. The soil our house was built on had not only settled, but it was literally washing away, causing our house to sink. From the outside, you wouldn't have noticed anything, but structurally our house was falling apart.

We knew we could no longer put it off. We were going to have to get the foundation repaired ASAP, because it was only going to get worse with time.

Your beliefs are the foundation that your life is built on.

If your life feels chaotic, unstable, or stagnant, the first place to check is your beliefs. Your beliefs are also called your thoughts, mindset, perspective, or inner voice. I will be using mindset and beliefs interchangeably. It's so important to understand what your beliefs are because they dictate your behaviors and your behaviors dictate your results. If you're not getting the results you want, you may be in need of a foundation repair.

Recognizing your beliefs can be challenging because they are so deeply ingrained that they create a blind spot. So instead, many people try to change their actions when they're not getting the results they want. That doesn't work. Even if you're able to change your behavior, it will be short-lived if you don't change the underlying belief.

Your behavior is a reflection of your beliefs.

Not all of your beliefs are bad. In fact, a lot of your beliefs may have gotten you to the level of success you're at now. The problem is that those same beliefs that got you where you are won't be able to get you to where you want to be.

Being a woman with vision will require you to outgrow yourself.

THE METAMORPHOSIS

It's kind of like a caterpillar. When a caterpillar is preparing to become a butterfly, its only job is to eat. Some caterpillars like Monarch caterpillars can eat up to 200 times their body weight. It consumes so much food because it needs to have enough energy to go through the metamorphosis process.

To make the transition from caterpillar to butterfly, you too need to make sure you are eating a lot. What do I mean? You want to make sure you are consuming information that's going to help build your beliefs and give you the energy and discipline to go through the transformation. This is where a lot of people get stuck because they don't consume enough information. As a result, they quit on the brink of their breakthrough.

When I was preparing to transition to full-time entrepreneurship, I set a goal to read ten books. I read sixteen. Trust me, I don't say that to brag. I knew that I was about to undergo a major change and I wanted to fill my head and my spirit with things that would be able to sustain me when things got a little shaky. And in full disclosure, I've needed everything I read in all sixteen of those books and them some!

But I didn't just read any books. I read books that aligned with my destination. I read books about marketing, finance, and entrepreneurship. I read books by people that are in the professional space I wanted to be in. And, I read my Word so that I could hear from God clearly. So be mindful of the books you read, the podcasts you listen to, television shows you watch, songs you jam to, who you follow on social media, and the people you surround yourself with. Are they feeding your beliefs positivity or are they feeding your beliefs negativity? What your second grade teacher said was true *You are what you eat.*

IT'S SHEDDING SEASON

As the caterpillar eats, it grows, but its skin doesn't expand with it. The caterpillar doesn't stop growing because it's scared of losing its skin. It doesn't give up on becoming a butterfly because it has to get rid of what has protected it up until now. It sheds it!

It eats, grows, and sheds its skin again. And again! And again! A caterpillar will shed its skin at least four or five times in the process.

You can't build a successful life or business on broken beliefs.

I want you to catch that. If you're going to go from the caterpillar stage to becoming a butterfly, you have to be willing to outgrow the mindsets, habits, and behaviors of a caterpillar. You must believe that where you are right now is just a phase and not your final destination. And you must be more committed to who you are becoming than who you have been. Recognize what beliefs no longer serve you and choose to let them go.

THE BELIEF GAP

Have you ever had a goal that you really wanted, but as hard as you tried, it seemed like you just couldn't break through? Or maybe you had a goal, but you weren't 100% confident that you could accomplish it?

This is what I call the Belief Gap™. The Belief Gap™ is what keeps most people from hitting their goals, even if they want it really bad.

The Belief Gap™ is the distance between your current mindset and the mindset you will need to achieve your goal.

Let me explain. When I was working as director of marketing, I was making $36,000 a year. I also had $36,000 a year beliefs and I did $36,000 a year behaviors.

- I traded time for money.
- I worked from 9:00 a.m.- 5:00 p.m.
- I wanted to have a consistent income.
- I wanted to generate leads, but I didn't want to sell.
- I thought selling was manipulative.
- I thought I was only worth $36,000 a year.

My goals, beliefs, and behaviors were in alignment. However, when I decided I wanted to make six figures, the beliefs and behaviors that got me to $36,000 weren't going to work. I had to change and elevate my way of thinking to align with who I needed to become to achieve that goal.

I had to let go of trading time for money and adopt a mindset that my clients were paying for the value I provided, not how much time I spent with them. I had to change my mindset that "sales" was a bad word, and I started believing that sales was just a conversation between two people. I had to let go of the idea of getting a consistent paycheck based on what the company thought I was worth, and embrace that I could get a higher income based on what I knew I was worth. This time in my life showed me that you don't manifest what you want...

You manifest your mindset.

Here's the kicker. I couldn't wait until I achieved the goal to start believing and behaving like someone who made six figures. I had to adopt the beliefs and actions BEFORE I reached the goal.

Once I started changing my mindset, I saw that my actions began to change as well. It wasn't enough for me to just think like someone who made six figures, I had to do what they did to get there.

Your goal might not be money-related, but the principle still applies. You must become the person that achieves the goal you want to accomplish before you accomplish it.

Here's the good news: Just like you had the power to create the beliefs you have now, you can create new ones. You can create a different story that is more empowering and fulfilling.

TAKE ACTION

What are three beliefs that have been holding you back?

1.

2.

3.

A woman with vision owns her truth!

CHAPTER 7

Elevating your Mindset

I always believe I can beat the best, achieve the best. I always see myself in the top position.

SERENA WILLIAMS

By now, you have probably recognized some self-limiting beliefs that have been holding you back, but you're still not sure how to change them.

The first step to elevate your mindset is to RECOGNIZE that something isn't working. This is probably the hardest step because our beliefs create blind spots that keep us from seeing a situation objectively.

These blind spots cause us to blame other people, things, and circumstances for our shortcomings, instead of taking personal responsibility.

People can't afford to buy...

No one ever supports me ...

I'm so busy I don't have time to...

I'm uncomfortable doing...

No one ever showed me how to...

RECOGNIZE

Until we recognize and accept ownership for our results, it's impossible to make progress. Here are some tips to help you recognize some of your subconscious beliefs:

- Write down the excuses you find yourself continually making.
- Watch what activities/tasks you avoid.
- Look at goals you keep recycling month after month and try to uncover your beliefs about that goal.

- Pay attention to how you feel. Your feelings are generally a clue to a thought you're having, whether conscious or subconscious.
- Journaling is a great tool to help you identify your internal dialogue.

REPLACE

After you recognize that your current belief system is holding you back, the next thing you want to do is to REPLACE your broken beliefs with something that supports who you want to become, and the goal you want to attain.

A few years ago, an event management company called me in complete hysteria. Their national sales meeting was a few days away, and one of the speakers canceled at the last minute. The VP of sales was frantic and wanted to know if I was available.

I had spoken for this company before, so I told them I would move a few meetings around so I could be available. The VP was relieved, and we began to go over the details such as date, time, location, and my topic. As we're going over the details, he mentions that I will be the second speaker and that lunch would be immediately following my presentation.

On the day of the sales meeting, I show up forty-five minutes early to get a feel for what the first speaker was covering. Before I even made it to the room, I could hear everyone laughing, clapping, and having an incredible time.

My nerves started to kick in. I thought to myself, *Crap! I was hoping I was going behind a lousy speaker (there's that insecurity I didn't know I had).* I opened the door and instantly my stomach dropped.

The VP of sales mentioned that there was someone going before me, but what he didn't tell me (and I didn't ask) was who the speaker was going to be. I knew this speaker. In fact, I had purchased one of his bestselling books, and he was internationally known. His books were sold at Barnes & Noble, Amazon, and airports. He had a team of people. AND...he had a fancy presentation with videos, graphics, and motivational quotes.

I slid into a chair in the back of the room and watched for ten minutes before escaping to the ladies' room. I needed to get myself together. How was I going to follow him?!

I hadn't written a book. Yes, my clients thought I was a sales guru, but let's be honest, I was not internationally known. I didn't have a fancy presentation. I didn't have a team of people. I was just a twenty-five-year-old woman with a flip chart that clearly had seen better days.

As I stood in the stall, something clicked. It was as if I became someone else and I started coaching myself on how to handle "the situation."

Looking back, I'm sure it was God reassuring me that He had already prepared me for this moment, but I couldn't see that then.

I took a deep breath, put my shoulders back, and my game face on. I started REPLACING my negative self-talk with beliefs that were going to support the outcome I wanted—killing this presentation.

Instead of thinking, *How am I going to follow him?* I changed it to *If he went first, that means that he was the opening act and I'm the headliner. I'm glad he warmed up the audience for me, so I'm not going in cold.*

One by one, all of these supportive beliefs started to flow in. That's because like attracts like. If I continued to think negative thoughts, I would have attracted more negative thoughts. By elevating my mindset and thinking positive thoughts, I attracted more positive thoughts. I walked in the bathroom scared and uncertain, but in less than five minutes I was able to shift my perspective and my presence.

When you elevate your mindset, you're able to see things you wouldn't usually be able to see. It's similar to being in an airplane. When you're in an airplane, the world doesn't change, but your perspective of it does and that makes all the difference.

Notice these new beliefs aren't rah-rah things I was telling myself. Everything I was telling myself was rooted in truth. He *was* warming up the crowd for me. He *was* going first. Therefore, he *was* the opening act.

REHEARSE

The third step to elevating your mindset is to rehearse your new belief out loud. Saying it out loud allows you to hear your own voice. When you hear your own voice, you begin to speak to your subconscious beliefs that might be in conflict with your new belief.

You might even feel like you're lying to yourself the first time you say this new belief out loud and that's okay. The more you do it, the more you will start to develop conviction in what you're saying, which is what you want. Conviction means you believe what you're saying in every fiber of you're being. Remember, you manifest your mindset, not what you memorize.

REINFORCE

I've never been a fan of affirmations. Or maybe I've never been a fan of how affirmations have been explained. In my experience, most affirmations are purely aspirational.

I am confident, brave, and strong.

I love everything about me.

I can reach any goal I set my mind to.

Yes, these make you feel good. Yes, they are motivational. But affirmations tend to miss the most critical piece to experience a real transformation — action!

To reinforce your new belief and truly elevate your mindset, you must take action in a way that aligns with what you said.

The most powerful way to affirm yourself is to take deliberate action that aligns with the highest version of yourself.

Let's dive deeper into this. Let's pretend every morning you rehearse the affirmation *I am confident, brave, and strong.* But every time you are presented with an opportunity to demonstrate your confidence, bravery, and strength, you run from it. What message does that reinforce to your subconscious? That you're really NOT confident, brave, nor strong.

Instead, let's turn this affirmation into a Power Belief. The difference between affirmations and power beliefs are...you guessed it, action! I call them Power Beliefs because action gives you power.

As women, we often underestimate how powerful we really are. You might even associate greed, control, or politics with the word *power*. But power doesn't have to be a dirty word. Power is also the ability to influence, and I want you to be able to take authority over your thoughts, so you can change your behavior. With that said, let's transform this affirmation into a Power Belief.

I am confident, brave, and strong becomes...

Every day I do things that challenge my comfort zone.

I say "Yes" to opportunities that will help me grow, even if I'm scared.

I seek out challenges that push me to become the person I want to be.

See the difference? This is an entirely different way of thinking and being. This approach even works on the more personal ones like *I am perfect as I am, and I love everything about me.*

Why don't you give it a shot? How could you add action to this affirmation, so it becomes a Power Belief?

Write it below:

_____

_____

_____

_____

_____

Here are some ideas:

I only speak kindly to myself, because that's all that's worthy of me.

I show myself grace every day.

I respect my body, thoughts, and space, and I accept nothing less from anybody else.

Maybe it's just me, but by the time I got to the third one, I was feeling myself. That's what Power

Beliefs do. They don't just make you feel good, they give you clarity on how you want to show up to yourself and the world.

The key that I want you to take away is that you have to be honest with yourself about your internal dialogue. If you have itty bitty beliefs wrapped in fear and insecurity, let's replace them with power beliefs. Then move those Power Beliefs from your head to your heart by repeating them out loud. You might even want to establish a routine of saying your Power Beliefs every morning as you get dressed, while you're driving to work, when you're at the gym, or before you go to bed. The more you say them, the quicker they will move from your conscious mind to your subconscious mind. And lastly, make sure that how you behave aligns with what you say you believe.

And just in case you didn't know, you are more powerful than you think. Or should I say, your power is in how you think.

TAKE ACTION

What's one non-supportive belief you will elevate?

What behaviors will you display to align with the new belief you will adopt?

A woman with vision believes in abundance!

CHAPTER 8

The Myths of Motivation

I learned a long time ago that there is something worse than missing the goal, and that's not pulling the trigger.

MIA HAMM

She took a deep breath and said, "I would like to make enough money in my side business to bring my mom from Africa, and be able to provide for both of us."

"So what would you like my help with?" I asked.

"I need help staying motivated."

I stared at the phone. Not in a judgmental way, but a little confused. How could you have a goal that seemed so meaningful but struggle to stay motivated? But the more coaching calls I did, the more people would pour out their hearts and aspirations, and then follow it up with how they needed help staying motivated.

After the third or fourth call, I knew I had to take a deeper dive and see what was really going on and that's when I discovered the *3 Myths of Motivation*.

MYTH 1: YOU HAVE TO FEEL MOTIVATED.

Do you *feel* inspired?

Do you *feel* excited?

Do you *feel* like taking action?

Can I be honest with you? Your goals don't care about how you feel. There will be days that you feel motivated and ready to walk through walls. There will also be days that you just want to lie in bed and watch re-runs. And if you're like me, there are days where you feel like both at the same time.

Feelings are fickle. If you solely rely on how you feel, you're going to be inconsistent. You can't afford to let your emotions be in the driver's seat.

You have to decide that what you want is more important than how you feel.

Is it more fun when you feel motivated? Perhaps. But what's really fun (and fulfilling) is when you finally accomplish something you've been wanting to do for months or maybe even years. That's fun!

PULL YOURSELF IN

Have you ever seen those videos where people are ziplining, and halfway through the zip line they start to slow down and they're dangling 100 feet in the air over the Amazon?

My husband and I witnessed this firsthand when we went ziplining on our honeymoon in St. Lucia. Fortunately, it wasn't one of us that got stuck! We were on the fourth zipline when a woman in our group got stuck three-fourths of the way through. Our guide instructed her to turn around and to pull herself in.

What happened? Did she lose motivation? No, she lost momentum! For many people, that's what it's like when they are working toward their goals. They start off feeling really motivated, and before they know it, they're halfway to their destination, and the excitement begins to wear off. They slow down and sometimes they even give up altogether. When that happens, you are you stuck in the Goal Setting Trap™ again, and you're virtually dangling 100 feet over the Amazon.

The challenge with being stuck is that it requires you to use more energy trying to "pull yourself in" than if you had maintained momentum.

You only need enough motivation to start, then focus on building momentum.

Webster defines momentum as a "strength or force gained by motion or by a series of events." The key to momentum is that it requires a *series* of events. Sometimes we take one step and then stop, because we didn't get the outcome we wanted. You can't build momentum doing something one time. You have to take consistent action.

So what do you do if you started but now you're stuck? You have to move.

Science was never "my thing," but something I've always remembered was Newton's Law of Motion. Newton's Law of Motion said an object in motion stays in motion. And an object at rest remains at rest. So the only way to get unstuck (and stay unstuck) is to move. Now, many people don't move because they're too concerned about making the "right" move. Let me reassure you, ANY movement is better than doing nothing.

MYTH 2: MOTIVATION IS EXTERNAL

We've all attended a women's empowerment event that had us on an emotional high. Two days later, after the glow wore off, the hashtag stopped trending, and you were back to business as usual, how did you feel?

I really want you to think about that.

How did you feel in comparison to when you left the event?

You probably weren't feeling the same level of excitement. Now, don't get me wrong. I love a good brunch or conference just as much as anybody else. I also believe there's incredible power when you're in a room of 5, 50, or 500 like-minded women all evolving to become their highest self.

However, what do you do when you don't have anybody rooting you on? How do you shift your negative thinking when you're doing the work, but you don't see the results? How do you keep going when obstacle after obstacle keeps coming up, and you feel like calling it quits? You have to look inside yourself.

Motivation is an inside job!

You are the only person that can truly motivate you—period. Other people can inspire you, they can hold you hold accountable, they can even cheer you on, but you're the only one that can motivate you.

When you embrace that you have the power to change how you feel in less than five seconds, you will be able to harness your emotions in extraordinary ways.

MYTH 3: MOTIVATION IS ONLY AN EMOTION

There's a great quote by the late Steve Jobs that says "If you are working on something that you really care about, you don't have to be pushed. The vision pulls you."

For many people, motivation is just an emotion. You *feel* motivated or you don't *feel* motivated. But motivation is more than that.

Motivation is your motive to take action.

So, if you are struggling to stay motivated, you might want to ask yourself: Am I working on something that I *really* care about? If not, stop investing time and energy into something that isn't meaningful to you. If it is something you care about, but you're struggling to stay motivated then there's a good chance that you haven't tapped into your CORE WHY. We'll talk about that next.

TAKE ACTION

What's one goal you're working on right now that you need to focus on building momentum?

What are three small steps you can take to start building momentum?

A woman with vision is a powerful force!

CHAPTER 9

What's your Motive?

The climb might be tough and challenging, but the view is worth it. There is a purpose for that pain; you just can't always see it right away.

VICTORIA ARLEN PAI

What's your motive? Why is this goal so important to you? Is it important enough that you're willing to go broke for it? Stay up late? Get up early? How would you feel if you didn't accomplish it?

These are all questions I ask myself as I'm getting to my motive. Going where you've never been or accomplishing something you've never done, is going to require you to do some things you don't know how to do and that you're scared of. If you don't know what your motive is, you are bound to get discouraged the first time you come across an obstacle.

It's not enough to have a goal if you don't know why you want it in the first place.

When I start asking my clients the questions mentioned above, many times they realize one of three things:

1.) They don't know what their motive is.

They hadn't really sat down and thought about what was driving them to pursue a particular goal. Maybe it was an idea they had, but if they were honest with themselves, they didn't *really* want it bad enough to do the work to make it happen, which is okay. It is okay (and I actually recommend) to let go of goals that aren't important to you. Life is too short to chase things that don't matter.

2.) Their motive was wrong.

In a world of curated Instagram feeds, Snapchat filters, and fearless #girlbosses, it's easy to fall into this trap (and I have). If you only want to accomplish specific goals because that's what society or social media says you need to have to appear successful, have influence, or be relevant, chances are your motives are out of alignment.

When you're out of alignment, you're not only out of your lane, but you're not in position for where God is taking you. Let that sit right there. When you are trying to do what everybody else is doing, and chasing what everybody else has, you're not in a position to receive what God has specifically for *you*. This is why you can try to do the same things that you've seen other people successfully do and not get the same result.

I've made this mistake. I had good content, good products, but my motives were off. My motivation was simple: I wanted to make money and lots of it, preferably as quickly as possible. Now, don't get me wrong. There's nothing wrong with wanting to make money. We live in a world where money is necessary, but there is something wrong when money is the only or primary motive. I had to shift my thinking (and my heart) to focus on impact and let God take care of my income. Was it challenging letting go of control? Yes. Was it necessary? Yes! Yes!

3.) They hadn't tapped into their real motive.

I'm sure, you've read other books that said you need to find your "Why." I want to take it to another level because knowing your "Why" isn't enough. When most people think of their "Why" it is very superficial.

I want to start my own business, *so I have more time to spend with my family.*

I want to pay off debt *so I can be financially independent.*

I want to write a book *to share my story.*

I call these "Whys" superficial for a couple of different reasons.

They're not personal.

Let's use paying off debt as an example. If you ask 100 people why they want to pay off debt,

95 people will say "because they want to be finan-cially independent." However, being financially independent means different things to different people. And, more important, WHY they want to be financially independent will be different.

Getting to the CORE WHY is about *why* your "Why" is important. When you start to uncover your CORE WHY, you begin to understand your true motive and you connect with your goals at a much deeper level.

There's no emotional connection.

There's no emotion attached to being financially independent. It's purely intellectual.

You create emotion by thinking about how it would feel to be financially independent and allow-ing yourself to feel that feeling now. You can also generate excitement by visualizing what you would be able to do (if you were financially independent) that you can't do right now.

Emotion creates impact.

For example, being financially independent might mean you would be able to provide scholarships to kids who grew up in a single-parent home. Visualize handing their parents a check with their child's name on it, as tears of gratitude stream down their face because they didn't know how they were going to send their child to school. Visualize seeing the students walk across the stage at their college graduation, debt-free because you were able to pay for their education. That feeling creates an imprint that serves as a reminder when you feel like waving the white flag.

CONNECTING TO YOUR CORE

Your CORE WHY is that internal, emotionally charged driving factor for pursuing a particular goal. The more difficult the goal, the more critical it is to connect to your CORE WHY. Your CORE WHY is what's going to keep you in the game and on track when it seems like nothing is working out. Your CORE WHY is what's going to help you make one more phone call, send one more email, write one more paragraph, do one more workout, and save one more dollar.

Anytime you find yourself struggling with motivation, remind yourself of your motive (CORE WHY) for taking action.

TAKE ACTION

Write down one of your goals.

Why is this goal important to you?

Why is your answer above important to you?

Why is your answer above important to you?

What did you learn about yourself or your motive?

A woman with vision lives with purpose!

CHAPTER 10

The " F " Words

> *I've learned that fear limits you and your vision. It serves as blinders to what may be just a few steps down the road for you. The journey is valuable, but believing in your talents, your abilities, and your self-worth can empower you to walk down an even brighter path. Transforming fear into freedom— how great is that?*

SOLEDAD O'BRIEN

It doesn't matter where you live. Every city has *that* street that always has bumper-to-bumper traffic, whether it's eight in the morning or two in the afternoon.

Where I live, that street is Spring Cypress. Anytime my GPS suggest Spring Cypress, I look for an alternate route, even if it's a route that's longer in distance.

Sometimes we try to take the same approach with fear. Instead of dealing with it head on, you try to find a shortcut or a back street, but fear doesn't work that way.

The only way to get pass fear is to go through it.

Fear is your body's natural alarm system that lets you know that you are in danger. Let's say you're walking to your car in a dimly lit parking garage and you hear footsteps following close behind, chances are fear or anxiety will begin to rise up.

You might respond by speeding up to create more distance between you and the person trailing behind. You might turn around to make eye contact. Or you might try to get to an area that is more visible. Either way, in that scenario, fear can actually keep you safe because it lets you know that something is wrong.

The problem with fear is when you feel that same anxiety about things that aren't life-threatening and you become paralyzed by it. In other words, the biggest problem with fear isn't fear itself, it's your response to it.

THE TRUTH

We all get nervous. We all second-guess ourselves from time to time. We all get a little anxiety when facing the unknown. That's okay. What's not okay is when you let fear keep you stuck. Instead of trying to become "fearless," focus on feeling the fear and leaning into it rather than running from it.

When I first started doing public speaking, I was terrified. The days leading up to a speaking engagement were gut-wrenching. My stomach would literally be in knots. I wish I could say that all my jitters have gone away over the last ten years, but it hasn't. It's gotten a lot better, but I still get a little nervous. Fortunately, it's only a few hours before I hit the stage versus days before.

What changed? Practice.

The more you do something, the more comfortable you become. There's no magic, just doing the work.

A LITTLE YARD WORK

I also learned to look at fear for what it is. It's an emotion. And as I mentioned before, your feelings aren't reliable. One of my Power Beliefs is that *I control my emotions, my emotions don't control me.* Because that is my mindset, when I feel fear beginning to develop, I address it. If you don't tackle fear immediately, it grows like weeds in your yard.

Weeds are opportunistic plants, which means they grow anywhere there's enough room to establish roots. That's also why weeds don't just show up in your yard, but they can grow through small cracks in the sidewalk or the street. Once it takes root, it spreads fast, stealing the nutrients from plants and grass that you actually want to grow.

Fear grows anywhere there's room.

Fear is the same way. It doesn't need a lot of room to do damage, it just needs a crack. It just needs a little insecurity. A little self-doubt. A hint of a victim mindset.

When you recognize fear, deal with it before it spreads. You don't want a feeling of fear to turn into a mindset (or spirit) of fear.

Now, you might be thinking, *There's nothing that I'm fearful of.* That's great! But also keep in mind that even if you don't have weeds visible in your yard right now, there are hundreds of seeds in your soil lying dormant until the right conditions present themselves. Similarly, you might not be struggling with fear now. However, you might be presented with an opportunity that is entirely outside of your comfort zone and instead of seizing the moment, you choose to play small.

Fear has a way of making you shrink or play it safe.

RESPONDING TO FEAR

After coaching hundreds of people over the last ten years, there are two common responses to fear that are counter-productive. The first one is the Self-Sabotage Spiral. The best way to explain the Self-Sabotage Spiral is to introduce you to Kara. Kara was an HR manager who was thinking about leaving her job to start her own HR consulting business. When I asked Kara what was holding her back, she responded that she didn't want to be homeless.

At first, I thought she was being sarcastic, but I soon realized she was serious. I asked her to explain to me what she meant.

She said that she was scared to quit her job because she didn't know if she was going to be able to get any clients. And if she wasn't able to get any clients, then she would have to get another job. But she wasn't sure if she would be able to get another job because all of her experience was in one industry, so then she wouldn't be able to pay her bills. Since she wouldn't be able to pay her bills, she would have to live in her car because she would be too embarrassed to tell anyone that she needed help. But her car wasn't in the best shape, so she would probably end up homeless on the street.

It's probably safe to say that we've all been Kara at some point. We've all talked ourselves out of what we want because of what we thought could go wrong. Remember, like attracts like. The moment you entertain a negative thought, you are feeding a weed that you don't want to grow. Not only that, but that weed then sucks the life out of what you're supposed to have, do, and become. Don't devote your time or energy to things or thoughts that you don't want to manifest.

MOUNTAIN CLIMBING

The second way I see people respond to fear is by creating a Mental Mountain.

Mental Mountains are built when fear causes you to become overwhelmed by all the things that you have to get done to bring your dream to fruition.

Let's use the previous scenario so you can see the difference. Instead of detailing everything you don't want to happen, you say, "I'm on the fence about leaving my job because ..."

I'll have to get a logo, but I don't know a graphic designer. I'd also have to register my business, but I don't even know where to start. I'd have to do social media, but I'm really a private person. I don't know how to price my services or determine what people are willing to pay. I don't know how to design a website, and the list goes on.

Every step is perceived as an obstacle instead of a typical step in the process. If you create Mental Mountains, you create so many barriers that you feel okay letting yourself off the hook for not taking action.

People who create Mental Mountains or go down Self-Sabotage Spirals are both reacting from the same place: fear.

This is also why it's so important to have your Power Beliefs that you have rehearsed and reinforced through action. That way you can sense sooner, rather than later, that you're about to go down a spiral or create a mountain.

THE OPPOSITE OF FEAR

If I asked you what the opposite of fear was, you might say being confident, fearless, or having faith. And while I think all of those are important, I want to give you a different perspective.

What if the opposite of fear was gratitude? What would happen if you started to have gratitude for the things that were causing you to be fearful? Just imagine how that would shift your whole perspective.

When I decided that I was going to leave my corporate job, I wasn't just leaving my job. We were selling our first home and relocating 250 miles away to a city where I had no network or connections. We were purchasing a home with zero guaranteed income, and we had a two-year-old son that was counting on us.

My initial response was "Let the spiral begin!"

But then I started to think about how blessed we were. Even though our first home had foundation issues, we were walking away with five figures in our pocket. I had a husband that was willing to sacrifice for me to pursue my dream. By relocating from Dallas to Houston, we would be closer to our family. Several people reached out to me about consulting work when I announced I was leaving my job. Past clients asked me what I was doing and how they could help. And if I didn't know how to do anything else, I knew how to sell!

When I began to be grateful, I realized that this was actually the best time to make a move! This was the best time to "start over" when our son was young. This was the best time to shift when I was still in my early 30s.

Gratitude changes your attitude.

THE SECOND "F" WORD IS FAILURE

In chapter 7, we talked about letting go of beliefs that no longer serve you. The concept of failure is an excellent example of a belief that you were taught as a kid that might be keeping you stuck as an adult.

In school, if you failed a test it was a reflection of what you did (or did not) learn. Failure was seen as a negative, and it came with repercussions in my house. However, as adults, failure is not the outcome of what we learned, it's *how* we learn.

Failure is feedback.

Think about that for a second. The only way to learn as an adult is by messing up and learning what not to do. You grow through trial and error. You get wiser by making mistakes.

If you keep holding on to the belief that failure means you're inadequate, you will never take the steps you need to take. As result, you will look up five years from now and be in the same place. Don't do that to yourself. God desires so much more for you than where you are.

Take the pressure off of yourself! I had to learn that it's okay not to be perfect. It's okay not to get it right the first time or the second time. It's okay to "mess up." You are not failing. You are learning! And everything you learn in this season will provide the foundation for your next season. Let me give you an example.

THE PLOT TWIST

One of my best friends, Andrea, got her undergraduate degree in biology. Andrea applied to a few dental schools, but she didn't get in.

Instead of sulking in disappointment, Andrea shifted and became a high school biology teacher. After eight years of teaching, she realized her desire to be in the medical field wasn't going to go away. It was now or never.

Andrea could have easily thought about the schools that rejected her the first go-around and decided that medical school wasn't for her, but she didn't. After eight years of teaching, she applied for medical school and was accepted!

Teaching for eight years taught Andrea how to take complex information and make it easy to understand, which is something she would have to do with patients. She learned how to connect with students who were guarded, which would allow her to communicate with patients who are scared, nervous, and hesitant to give her the information she needs to care for them properly. She learned how to study and break information down, which helped her navigate medical school.

Andrea was able to take everything she learned, while being a teacher, to help her become an exceptional nurse. In other words, her failure and rejection were actually her training ground for her purpose.

THE BUCK STOPS HERE

You are capable of more than what you've been settling for. There are so many ideas and ambitions bottled up inside of you, but you let fear talk you out of what is rightfully yours. No more!

Reignite all those dreams that you've buried, and go after them with everything you have. The buck stops here! Every no, rejection, and failure you have experienced was preparing you for where God is taking you. It's only up from here!

TAKE ACTION

What decisions have been on hold because you've been too scared to make a move?

Now, take three minutes and just write how grateful you are for the opportunity, idea, or decision.

A woman with vision does it scared!

CHAPTER 11

Who Must You Become?

Don't be afraid. Be focused. Be determined.
Be hopeful. Be empowered.

MICHELLE OBAMA

The best goals are the ones you have to grow into, because they stretch you and force you to level up. They make you dig deeper and dream bigger. They make you want to be better and go harder. They make you step up and lean in. They make you scared one moment and optimistic the next.

If you have a goal that doesn't challenge you to rise to the occasion, chances are it's not a goal, it's just a to-do list item.

Remember *real* goals make you grow. So, I have a question for you.

Who must you become to reach your goals?

This was a challenging question for me because I grew up with messages like "don't change," "don't forget where you come from," and "don't act brand new." So, I wrestled with wanting to better myself, but not wanting to make people feel like I thought I was better than them. I also believed that if I just worked hard, I'd get there, eventually. I was scared to take an inward look at myself to see what about me was getting in the way of my own success.

But then I had to accept the reality that who I was, at that very moment, was incapable of achieving what I desired, otherwise, I would have already done it.

The shift I wanted to experience was going to have to begin with me shifting my way of thinking, being, and doing. And the same is true for you.

Let me give you an example. Before writing this book, I would struggle just trying to come up with an Instagram caption. So the thought of writing thousands of words to fill a book was terrifying. However, when I made the commitment that I was going to do it, I immediately thought about the habits and beliefs that I would need to change. It's not that my habits and beliefs were necessarily wrong, but they weren't going to help me write a book in 30 days.

I had to create a behavior of blocking out writing time, staying up after my husband and son went to sleep, only checking emails after lunch, so it wouldn't eat into my writing time (pun intended), and scheduling my social media, so I wouldn't be distracted by it.

I also had to elevate my beliefs and start thinking like a published author. Since public speaking is something I love to do, one of my Power Beliefs was *Writing is just talking on paper.* It doesn't sound fancy, but when I would get writer's block, this Power Belief reminded me to write what I would say if I were on stage. This Power Belief alone helped me write 20,000+ words, and that's after cutting a whole chapter out.

The point is that I had to think and behave like an author if I wanted to be an author.

So back to you, who must you become to reach your goals?

Give yourself permission to become.

Depending on where you are now and where you want to be, the answer to that question will vary. Yet there are five universal qualities that you want to make sure you develop as a woman with vision.

As I share each quality, take a personal inventory of which ones you have mastered and which ones you need to focus on.

DECISIVENESS

I was speaking at an executive breakfast in Baltimore a while back. At the end of my presentation, a woman came up to me (she was also the only woman there) and she told me how much I had inspired her. She was an executive at her job, but she wanted to do public speaking on the side to share how she went from growing up in the projects to getting her MBA and helping run one of the largest companies in Baltimore.

Her story almost had me in tears. I asked her what was keeping her from doing it. She said the only thing that was holding her back was her website. She had been working on her site for over a year, and she was no further today than she was a year ago. So you know I had to dig a little more.

She couldn't decide on her logo, font, header picture, speaking topics, or audience. After a little more probing, I helped her realize that her biggest problem wasn't that she didn't know what to do or what she wanted, but she was scared of making the wrong decision. As a result, she made no decisions.

As a woman with vision, you have to be comfortable making a decision and course correcting as you go. The last thing you want to do is get bogged down every time you have to make a decision.

Indecisiveness has an opportunity cost...

Because the time and energy you keep putting into the same thing could have been used toward something far more productive. Lastly, the longer it takes you to make a decision, the harder it becomes.

Here are a couple of things that have helped me become more decisive:

Reduce the number of options.

The more options you give yourself, the more difficult it is to make a decision. If possible, only give yourself two choices to pick from.

Give yourself a deadline.

If you have a big decision that you have been wrestling with, set a deadline to make the decision and stick to the deadline.

Practice every day.

Look for opportunities in your daily routine to practice making decisions quicker. For example, if you have a hard time deciding what to order at a restaurant, force yourself to make a decision. Can't choose what to wear to work today? Grab your go-to outfit and move on. If you struggle to determine what goal you should work on first, just pick one and start working on it.

TAKE RISKS

We often use the term "comfort zone" to describe the things that feel most natural to us. It may be in your comfort zone to go to a networking event and walk up to complete strangers and start a conversation with no hesitation. I, on the other hand, may feel nervous or anxious at just the *thought* of having to talk to someone that I don't know.

Sometimes you might feel as though your comfort zone is set in stone, but it's not. You created your comfort zone, therefore, you have the power to change it, expand it, or remove it altogether.

Your comfort zone is nothing more than self-imposed limitations.

Your comfort zone is a *psychological* barrier, but what trips us up is the *physical* response. When you feel your hands sweating, your heart beating fast, or your mouth turning into the Sahara Desert, it reinforces the idea that you are doing something dangerous. However, you can control and reverse your physical response by changing the story you have going on in your head.

The easiest way to change the story is to ask yourself questions! Asking yourself questions helps to pull out the logical, problem-solving part of your brain versus being on a runaway train with your amygdala, which is the part of the brain that controls your emotions.

Here are some questions you can ask yourself when you're nervous about doing something that is outside of your comfort zone:

- *What am I really nervous about?*
- *What scares me the most about_____?*
- *What evidence do I have to justify the way I'm feeling?*
- *What can I do to be better prepared for _____?*
- *What's the ideal outcome I'm looking for?*
- *What can I do to increase my chances of getting that outcome?*
- *How do I really want to feel? How can I feel that way instead?*
- *If I felt confident doing _____, what actions would I take?*
- *How can I leverage my strengths to help me feel more confident about _____?*

After a few minutes of asking yourself questions, you will see a significant change in your physical response. Your breathing will slow down, your hands will become less clammy, and it won't feel like you've been chewing on sandpaper.

Keep in mind that expanding your comfort zone isn't about making massive changes all at once. It's about creating a habit of doing small things that help you grow.

Remember, you control your emotions, your emotions don't control you!

RESILIENT

One day I was on the online dictionary, and the "Word of the Day" popped up in the right sidebar. The word was *regardless*.

regardless, adjective

re·gard·less | \ri-'gärd-ləs

despite everything

When I saw that on my screen, I almost fell out of my chair. I don't know if it was because of everything I was going through at the time or what, but it hit me over the head like a two-by-four.

I made a decision that day that I was going to adopt a spirit of *regardless,* despite everything. Despite delays, denials, obstacles, circumstances, haters, and even my own insecurities, I am going to pursue the vision God gave me.

When challenges come up, and they will, I want you to say to yourself *REGARDLESS!* Don't allow yourself to be so easily discouraged when you don't get the results you're looking for. Don't throw in the towel because you tried something once and it didn't go your way. So what if other people seem to be going faster than you. Their journey isn't your journey!

It doesn't matter how many times you have tried and failed before this very moment. People are counting on you to stick it out this time. You are counting on you to stick it out this time!

FOCUS

Grab the pen that you're taking notes with and flip it where the tip of the pen is pointed toward the ceiling. Hold it an inch from your nose and stare at the tip of the pen. What happened?

When you focus on the tip of the pen, everything else should get blurry. That's what it's like when you practice focusing. Instantly you recognize what's important and what's just a distraction.

For many, myself included, staying focused is a constant struggle because there's so much vying for your attention. And sometimes it's not even about being able to focus, it's about making sure you're focused on the things that honestly matter.

Choose to do less

Focus on completing one task before starting another. Yes, that means you need to stop trying to multitask. Trying to multitask is like opening multiple browsers on your computer and then wondering why it's running slow. Although you feel like you're being productive, you're really just switching your attention from one thing to another. Not only is that counter-productive, but it actually increases your risk of making mistakes.

Your attention must follow your intention.

Remember to begin your day by asking yourself *What's the single most critical thing I have to get done today?*

Tackle that one thing, and once you're done, ask yourself that same question again. Keep doing that until you're done for the day. What's really amazing about asking that question is the number one priority always rises to the top.

This also applies to your goals. Don't set yourself up for failure by trying to accomplish too many goals at the same time, unless being frustrated and overwhelmed is your thing. Focus on no more than three goals at any one time, and that's if you're already really disciplined. When it comes to your goals for the year, don't pick more than ten. You can always add more, but you don't want to start with twenty.

LEARNER

Have you ever heard the saying "Learners are earners?" I don't remember the first time I heard someone say it, but I do remember thinking that it sounded pretty cheesy. But as cheesy as it sounds, it's true.

In my previous career doing sales training and consulting, one of the services we offered was recruiting. Whenever I was interviewing a candidate, I would always ask the candidate this question: *What's the last investment you made in your own personal or professional development?*

Nine out of ten times if the candidate couldn't answer within five seconds, the candidate did not move forward in the hiring process. Now, I know that might sound harsh. But the fact is, successful people make learning a habit.

Whether it's reading a book, listening to a podcast, taking a course, meeting with a mentor, or joining a mastermind, winners have a hunger for information. And *really* successful people not only seek out information, but they internalize it, and then implement it so they get better results.

Look at your goals and see what skills you need to learn to make them happen, and then create a personal development budget that you can pull from to invest in yourself and your goal.

You can't get rich being cheap.

TEACH ME HOW TO DOUGIE

YouTube has videos on just about anything you want to learn how to do. However, sometimes it is worth paying to learn from someone on a more personal level. When I was preparing to leave my job, I invested over $3,000 in courses and programs so I could fast track my goals. I'm not saying that you need or should pay that much, but what I am saying is that DIY-ing everything isn't always the best idea. What you save in money, you spend in time... and time is money.

What if your goal isn't monetary? You still can't get rich being cheap. You can't have a marriage rich in love and understanding without investing time and money into it. You can't have a life rich in peace without investing energy and effort into your spiritual development. You can't be in the best physical shape eating cheap, processed food.

If you're serious about your goals, it will cost you something!

Being a woman with vision means you are continually evolving. Who you are today should be different than who you'll become tomorrow. That doesn't mean you lose the essence of who you are or what you value, but instead, you work to make sure that how you live and show up in the world actually honors that.

TAKE ACTION

What's the last investment you made in your own personal or professional development?

What's one investment you need to make in your personal or professional development?

A woman with vision is always evolving!

CHAPTER 12

Go To Work!

Be true to yourself ... Always.

MOM

Throughout this book, we talked about embracing your shadow—the bigger version of yourself—instead of running from it. I gave you a behind-the-scenes look at the Goal Setting Trap™ and helped you understand why you've suffered from Start-Stop Syndrome up until now.

You also learned the difference between vision and goals, and why it's important to make sure the two are in alignment as much as possible. I also mentioned that you need to reward yourself as you achieve milestones, so you don't lose sight of the bigger picture.

I broke down the four areas that you need to focus on if you want to move from setting goals to slaying them ... *just as a reminder it was clarity, planning, execution, and mindset.* We did a deep-dive on changing your internal dialogue, looking at both The Belief Gap™ and the four-step process to recognize, replace, rehearse, and reinforce to elevate your mindset.

Then you learned that motivation is way more than just an emotion, it's about discovering your motive to take action. You also learned that you only need enough motivation to start, then you want to focus on building momentum by taking action every day.

From there, we walked through the "F" words: fear and failure. And finally, I shared the five characteristics of a woman with vision.

PROTECT YOUR VISION

When I first had my son, I was the germ police. You could not hold him without me seeing you wash your hands, there had to be a blanket between his skin and your clothes, and kissing him was completely out of the question. As his mother, it was my job to protect him until he developed a resistance to things we often take for granted. The same is true for your vision. You must protect your vision, especially in the infancy stage. That means you can't share your goals, dreams, and ambitions with everyone. And sometimes that includes the people closest to you.

CANDY CRUNCHING COCONUT LOVERS

Growing up, one of my favorite childhood games was telephone. Telephone was when all of your friends would sit in a circle and someone would whisper a phrase in the person's ear sitting next to them, and you would continue to pass the message around the circle. It didn't matter if you had five people or fifteen people, the phrase always changed.

Sometimes it changed on accident because someone genuinely misunderstood what the person next to them said. Other times, it was altered on purpose. In this case, someone intentionally added their own stamp so it would be different.

In the past, you may have treated your goals like a game of telephone. God gave you a vision or there was a goal you had, and you shared it with your friends and family.

You fully expected them to be as excited as you were and to encourage you to make it happen, but instead, they changed the message and started asking you a bunch of questions that made you second-guess yourself.

Was that really God?

Do I have time to get that done?

Maybe I am thinking too big.

Since you were confused, you decided you should run it by someone else, and you were met with the same skepticism. Three people later, you're thoroughly convinced that you must have misheard God, so you go back and pray for clarity ... again.

Sharing your goals with people who haven't accomplished what it is you're working toward or who don't share the same mindset, will always lead to frustration.

You cannot blame someone for not having the capacity to appreciate the magnitude of your goals. Instead, choose not to put them in that position by keeping it to yourself. Or, only sharing it with people that can help you get closer to what it is you're trying to achieve.

Everyone doesn't need to know everything.

That doesn't mean that you can't share your goal with them eventually, but I would avoid it in the beginning.

Secondly, doubt is highly contagious, and if you listen to it long enough, you will catch it. The moment you hear doubt or fear from someone else, politely excuse yourself from the conversation. Do not ask questions or get defensive, just choose not to participate further.

Lastly, don't waste precious energy trying to prove people. Instead, focus your energy on proving it to yourself that you could do it.

PROTECT YOUR VISION FROM YOURSELF

Sometimes it isn't other people you have to worry about, it's you. Learn to be kind to yourself and show yourself grace. Speak blessings over your future, not negativity. When you talk about what you don't know or what you don't have, you are operating from a place of lack. Just as like attracts like, lack attracts lack. Believe that everything you need, you already have, and God will make up the difference.

Know that you are capable and qualified. Let me repeat that: *You are capable and qualified!* Yes, you!

You are capable and qualified!

You don't need anyone else's validation. When you seek out the validation and approval of other people, it's usually because you haven't validated or approved yourself. Whether you use affirmations, scriptures, or Power Beliefs, make sure you validate yourself on a daily basis.

Be grateful for where you are and learn from every experience that life brings your way. Tackle each day with the assurance that if you do the work, you will reap the reward. Trust the process. Don't just learn from failure, embrace it because failure isn't the opposite of success, it's part of it.

Don't get wrapped up in comparing yourself to other people and where they are in their journey. You have no idea what price they have paid to get where they are, and you have no idea where they are headed. Be so focused on your own goals that you don't have time to waste watching what someone else is doing.

FEED YOUR VISION

Make time to work on your goals at least sixty minutes every day. No excuses!

If you don't feed your vision, it will die.

Be as committed to your own goals as you are to other people. Plus, when you go after your dreams, you are more fulfilled, and it changes how you show up to your friends, family, coworkers, and employees.

WHO DO YOU KNOW?

One of the things I often hear from women is that they feel alone. They don't feel like they have anyone in their corner. Or they don't have a circle of like-minded women who are trying to elevate themselves.

My suggestion is always the same: be what you need for someone else. Initially, that might sound backward. How is helping someone else going to help you? But when you give, it frees up space for you to receive.

You know another woman who needs to be reminded of who she is and the power that lies within. Whether it's through social media, teaching the lessons you've learned, or even buying a copy of this book to give to her, pass this message along. Let your life and courage be the example that someone else needs to see.

You can also join A Woman With Vision Facebook group. It is safe place where you can get the encouragement, support, and accountability to implement what you've learned in this book. Just remember to be a giver, and not a taker. Give the advice, feedback, and support that you'd like to receive, and you will always get a return.

WHEN LIFE HAPPENS

Life is going to happen, that's a given. Being a woman with vision allows you to know and believe that despite what you might be facing, the best is yet to come.

There isn't a better example of this than my friend, Brisa. Four months before her 27th birthday, Brisa was diagnosed with thyroid cancer. All of sudden, her life, as she knew it, was replaced with doctor visits, tests, and pills to prepare her body for the battle that lied ahead. Realizing how fragile life was, Brisa decided that she could no longer live life just going through the motions. She was going to do everything she had been putting off, and she did!

A month after receiving her diagnosis, Brisa had surgery to remove the cancer, followed by radiation two months later. As someone who watched Brisa go through her journey, there was one thing that stood out to me. She never played the victim. Was she scared? Yes! Did it suck?! Yes! But she wasn't going to let cancer win. I am happy to report that Brisa is cancer-free, and she had a fantastic wedding, just three weeks after radiation.

If you're in that place right now, where you've lost your mojo, and you've been sitting on the sidelines because life threw you a curveball, this is the sign you've been praying for. You never know what life is going to bring, but you can choose how you're going to respond to it.

Get back in the game, sis! The world needs you to show up. You need you to show up!

NEXT STEPS

At this point, you're probably thinking one of two things: Where do I start? Or, this is all great, but can I really do this?

Let me begin by addressing the latter. Yes, you can absolutely do this! And, I don't say that just to make you feel good. I say that because I've been where you are. I've had moments where I felt stuck, and it seemed like everything was stacking up at once, and I just couldn't catch a break. There were times where I didn't even try because I didn't want to experience the disappointment of achieving something, only to turn around and lose it. And, I know what it's like to cheer other people on while secretly battling my own inner critic who *constantly* tries to remind me of past failures.

But, there's a reason you bought this book. You have that same desire for more fulfillment that I had five years ago, and you know that God has so much more for you than just getting by. Now it's up to you to accept that you *deserve* better. This was a tough one for me. I wanted better, but I didn't think I *deserved* better.

When I started believing I deserved better, everything began to change. I began to attract people who poured into me in ways that I didn't even know I needed. Business opportunities started seeking me out versus me having to try to get in front of them. I was able to hear God in a way that I hadn't been able to hear Him before. I was able to leave a job that was literally making me sick. And, achieving my goals became fun instead of a constant grind.

My hope is that you commit to yourself, your future, and the vision God has shown you so that you too can experience the power that comes from being a woman with vision.

YOUR TURN

I have literally peeled back the cover on everything that's been keeping you from accomplishing the goals and dreams God has given you. However, you can't start changing everything at once. The first thing you want to start with is prayer.

That's probably not what you were expecting. But the reality is that as women we often put everyone and everything else before ourselves. As a result, sometimes we don't even know what we want. Or, we want so many different things that we have no idea where to begin. Within the next 24 hours find 20-30 minutes where you just sit and ask God, *What do you desire for me? What's the bigger version of myself? What should I be focused on?* And then, just listen. You will be amazed by the clarity you get by just putting some pause in your day.

The second thing is to remember that it isn't inspiration that creates a transformation, it's what you do with it. You have to take everything you've learned and get it out of your head and into your heart. What I mean by that is that you have to internalize and believe that it will work for you. Once you internalize it in your heart, make sure it moves into your hands in the form of action. It is only through consistent action that it will become habit, and you'll experience a true breakthrough.

Last, but not least, on your journey to becoming a woman with vision, be patient with yourself as you evolve. Know that even in the most challenging times, you always have someone out there rooting for you.

For me, this is more than just a book, this is my life's work. Now, go do yours!

Much Success,

Lareal Lipkins
Wife, Mother, Visionary, Author

Acknowledgments

This is by far the hardest part to write, because there are no words to describe my gratitude.

I have been blessed with a fantastic support system that I'm eternally grateful for.

First things first, none of this would have been possible without God. I have always had a relationship with God, but I haven't always surrendered my will to Him. This year is the year of surrender. Whatever He says to do, I'm doing—no questions asked. I knew I wanted to write a book someday, but it wasn't even on my radar right now. I definitely didn't think I would write a book in less than a month, but when it's God, it's God! I'm just grateful that He let me his coauthor.

To my hubby, partner in crime, and love of my life, I thank you from the bottom of my heart. I really don't know how you put up with me and all my ideas, but I'm glad you do. I know for sure there's no way I could have written this book without you. You gave me the time I needed to write, you were a sounding board for all the thoughts running through my head, and you reassured me that if I could write as much as I talk, I could fill a thousand pages. Lol!

Deuce, thank you for choosing me to be your mommy. From the moment we found out you were coming, you made me step up my game. I hope one day you'll look back at this and know that everything we did was for you.

Mom, where do I even begin? When I first started Vision Boards Over Brunch in 2015, you not only cooked all the food, you bought a ticket because you said that you wanted to sow a seed. It's harvest time! Thank you for your constant and unwavering support! I wouldn't be the woman I am today, had it not been for your example.

Dad, when I told you I was thinking about quitting my job, your response was priceless. You said, "Great! Make it happen!" That meant the world to me, because I had already secretly quit my job. Thank you for always believing in me, and I pray that I have made you proud.

Bacardi and Ananias, growing up with an older brother and younger brother taught me how to be tough (thanks Bacardi), and how to nurture (thanks Ananias). Growing up, I didn't realize how much I would need both of those to become the woman I am today. I love you both with all my heart!

Candace, thank you so much for contributing to this book. When I reached out to you about writing a poem, you didn't hesitate. Your words captured the essence of this book so beautifully, and I can't thank you enough!

Kim, Kim, Kim! I don't know how you do it, but you always say just the right thing at just the right time. I don't even have to say anything and you jump in and ask, "What do you need?" "How can I help?" You are the definition of ride-or-die, and I love you for that!

Brisa, you get me! We are two sides of the same coin. Thank you for always giving me the space to be who I am—the good, the bad, and the petty! Lol! When I was nervous about taking the leap, not only did you help me realize my power, you made the leap first. You are amazing, and I'm glad to call you my friend. Yep, it's in writing.

Tierra, I tell you all the time how much you inspire me! What I haven't told you is that you were the first person to make me realize and accept my purpose. From the beginning, you've been right there cheering me on. I needed that more than you'll ever know.

F.A.V.E: Andrea, Elisha, Essence. Wow! This could be a whole book in itself. I am truly blessed to be able to call you all my friends and my sisters. Andrea, thank you for showing me what it looks like to go all in for what you want. Watching the sacrifices you've made to follow your dream not only changed my life, it saved it. Elisha, for the last twenty years, you've always had my back. Thank you for the texts, DMs, calls, and prayers. You keep me going when I don't see the light at the end of the tunnel! Essence, thank you for always being honest with me. Our conversations make me look at myself and want to become better: a better wife, a better mother, a better woman, and a better friend.

22 Pearls of Synergy, when I told you I was moving to Houston, each and every one of you rallied behind me. I love you all and I'm so grateful for the support.

I owe a huge thank you to everyone that worked on this book. Lakia "LB" Brandenburg, you are best editor I could have ever asked for. Melarie Odelusi at Mauve Paper Co., thank you for taking my rough sketches and turning them into beautiful illustrations. Sherilyn Bennet, you brought the cover to life in a way I couldn't have even imagined. Ronnee at Belaan Beauty, thank you for always dolling me up. And to my amazing husband, who captured the cover photo, thank you for always bringing out the best in me!

Lastly, but certainly not least, a huge thank you goes to you! Your support of this book is a reminder to me that I'm on the right path. Thank you for allowing me to be transparent and entrusting me to speak into your life.

Speaking Request

Below are some of L'areal's most requested topics:

COMPANIES

- Leading With Vision
- Elevate Your Mindset: How to Position Yourself for Success
- Corporate Vision: The Key to Engagement
- Vision Board Workshops + Team Building

CONFERENCES + COLLEGES

- Becoming A Woman With Vision
- Vision: Why Some People Win & Others Don't
- Elevate Your Mindset: The Real Key to Leveling Up
- Reigniting Your Dreams

CHURCHES

- Becoming A Woman With Vision
- Elevate Your Mindset: Who did God Say You Are?
- Reigniting Your Dreams

L'areal can tailor a talk for your specific group. For booking, please email Lareal@AWomanWithVision.com

JOIN OUR GROUP ON
Facebook

A Woman With Vision Facebook Group is a safe place where you can find support, encouragement, and accountability on your journey!

Get weekly tips
Share your wins
Ask questions + Get feedback
Get advance notice on programs

To join, go to www.Facebook.com and search for **A Woman With Vision** in Groups!

A Woman With Vision Masterclass is a self-paced course designed specifically for women who want to fast track their results.

In addition to eight detailed video modules, you get access to templates, a digital workbook for immediate access, and a hard copy workbook to plan and track your goals for the next twelve months.

For more info visit:
www.AWomanWithVision.com/masterclass

About the Author

L'areal Lipkins is a speaker and success strategist who helps women, who have big dreams, goals, and ambitions, get from where they are to where they want to be. Through her online programs, coaching, and live events, L'areal has helped thousands of women elevate their mindset and their lives.

Before starting Lipkins Consulting Group full-time, L'areal did sales training and consulting for one of the largest sales training companies in the world for nearly a decade. Today, she combines her corporate experience and personal journey to inspire audiences worldwide.

L'areal is a proud member of Delta Sigma Theta Sorority, Inc. and lives in Houston, TX with her husband, son, and dog, Bella.

CPSIA information can be obtained
at www.ICGtesting.com
Printed in the USA
LVHW051551290122
709584LV00012B/1402